CHILDREN'S

SASKATCHEWAN

SASKATCHEWAN

Photographs by Menno Fieguth

Introduction by C. Irwin McIntosh
Foreword by Allan Blakeney

CORRECTIONS

Introduction, para. 3:
Even though it has less than five per cent of Canada's population, Saskatchewan contains forty-three per cent of its arable land, which may explain why it has twenty-three per cent of the nation's highway systems.

Plate 24:
For Government House *read*
Northwest Territorial Assembly Building.

Plate 29:
For Wasana *read* Wascana.

Toronto
OXFORD UNIVERSITY PRESS
1980

To Joyce, Cheryl, and Debbie

Grateful acknowledgement is hereby made to the
Saskatchewan Arts Board for financial assistance, at a time
when that help was most needed, toward my project of
photographing Saskatchewan.

MF

Designed by FORTUNATO AGLIALORO

© Oxford University Press (Canadian Branch) 1980
ISBN 0-19-540355-X

1 2 3 4 - 3 2 1 0

Printed in Hong Kong by
EVERBEST PRINTING COMPANY LIMITED

FOREWORD

The landscape of Saskatchewan is as infinite and varied as its people.
From its frozen lakes and vast northern forests to the tabletop
of its southern prairie, Saskatchewan offers the photographer
a movable feast of contrasts. Its timeless and abiding nature
gives strength and encouragement to the struggles, dreams,
and achievements of all who live here.

Allan Blakeney
Premier

INTRODUCTION

This is Saskatchewan.

A conundrum to farm pioneers, economists, geologists, and to many generations of politicians, Saskatchewan is a land loved by our people for its beauty, diversity, and opportunity.

Even though it has less than five per cent of Canada's population, Saskatchewan contains forty-three per cent of the nation's highway systems. The province is by far the biggest producer of our country's two largest food crops, wheat and rape. These riches are a great tribute to the productivity of our 69,000 farms.

It is the land, a few inches of precarious top soil, that has dominated Saskatchewan life. For almost seventy-five years the province has experienced the ups and downs of a one-crop wheat economy. However, cut-crop diversification, livestock production, and new technology have revolutionized farming in Saskatchewan.

Not only the top soil but what lies under it has changed Saskatchewan life. When geologists were searching for oil in the fifties they found the world's richest and largest strata of potash, a key ingredient for much of the world's fertilizer. Though we do not need it for our own soil, it is currently providing us with a billion-dollar-a-year industry.

Oil was eventually found in Saskatchewan, but many of the reserves, and especially those in the Lloydminster region of western Saskatchewan, were of such a nature that it has only now become worthwhile to extract them for the needs of an energy-hungry nation. Today the province provides some eleven per cent of Canada's output.

The pioneers along the American border found a rolling, almost treeless grassland, with outcrops of lignite coal here and there. They mined the coal and carted it home in wagons to keep their cabins warm during our long winters. Today at Estevan and Coronach huge coal beds are being exploited to provide thermal generation of electricity to meet the growing fuel demands of industry across the province.

Saskatchewan is not simply prairie from horizon to horizon. It is a land of infinite variety. In the southwestern corner, not far from Swift Current and just below the cowtown of Maple Creek, the Cypress Hills are as high above sea level as Banff. The hills are a haven not only for ranchers but for moose, elk, and deer; in the lowlands that roll up to the forested hills, antelope range across the open prairie.

The parklands, between the prairies and the Precambrian Shield, have a charm of their own at The Battlefords, where the colourful valleys of the Battle and North Saskatchewan Rivers join. Here the tourist can view a rolling landscape of poplar bluffs, rivers, and lakes that sweeps from prairie to forest as far north as the sand dunes on the south shore of Lake Athabasca — one of the ten largest freshwater lakes on earth.

At Prince Albert, where the North and South Saskatchewan Rivers meet, a giant pulp mill makes this northern city the hub of the province's timber industry. Nipawin, on the northern rim of the rich farm land of the Carrot River Valley, boasts a rapeseed oil refinery that also manufactures margarine.

The North is another land again. Where the farmlands end, the timber resources begin, stretching north to the mighty Churchill, which leads to a series of great lakes and rivers and some of the finest canoeing, angling, and hunting country in North America.

More than half of Saskatchewan's northland is dominated by the hard rock of the Precambrian Shield. For generations geologists searched for precious ore in this rugged wilderness, neglecting the bland sandstone formations that arc around the south shore of Lake Athabasca. They neglect them no longer. Less than a decade ago geologists with a French exploration company located a large boulder that showed remarkable concentrations of uranium ore. The Cluff Lake discovery promises to change the face of the North. Today new roads are being pushed towards this fragile wilderness and its many rich uranium deposits.

And what of Saskatchewan's people? At the turn of the century they came from the four corners of the world. Saskatchewan is unlike any of the other provinces. Descendants of the original British and French settlers make up less than half of our population. Our province is a mosaic of peoples that includes a host of Germans, Ukrainians, Polish, Dutch, and Scandinavians and lesser numbers of Hungarians, Russians, Rumanians, Assyrians, Greeks, Italians, and Americans. Our Indian and Métis populations have been stirred by a new generation of leaders.

In 1980 Saskatchewan celebrates its seventy-fifth anniversary as a province of Canada. Since it was founded in 1905 it has been tempered by frost, drought, flood, and war. Few peoples have had to undergo such trials and tribulations as our pioneers. The prairies were bleak, lonely, and forbidding. Today that is a memory. Rural electrification has spread the amenities of life throughout this broad land. Though the population is widely scattered, a network of modern provincial and rural roads has brought security and comfort to yesterday's wilderness.

Urban communities large and small have also been enriched by the province's resource and agricultural wealth.

The people of Regina watch our capital city soar into the sky with new construction of office and residential towers. Regina is the seat of government and the home of many Crown corporations and the province's steel industry.

Saskatoon is a booming centre of the potash and uranium industries, but its people worry that their handsome river city will grow too quickly to maintain the quality of life they have come to cherish.

Yet the real wonder of industrial expansion in Saskatchewan may be epitomized by the growth of smaller cities, such as Yorkton. Here the inventiveness of our farmers has sparked several farm-equipment companies in the production of specialized machines for prairie agriculture that are now exported around the world.

Moose Jaw is vitalized by the province's only armed-forces training base. Every second year the Canadian Forces Base Moose Jaw has one of the largest air shows in Canada, drawing some 100,000 visitors from across the prairies.

We are a thinking, political people. Through need we have conceived many new political and economic ideas. Our producer- and consumer-owned co-operatives are among the largest in Canada. Our governments have created numerous Crown corporations—expressions of a demand for public control of the province's economic future. Because of the great mark the Depression and drought left upon us, the people of Saskatchewan share a genuine feeling of brotherhood. That spirit gave us the first hospitalization and medicare plans in North America.

The pictures in this book have a quality that tells better than I can of the richness of Saskatchewan life. Photographer Menno Fieguth—who was born at Tiefengrund, just north of beautiful Saskatoon—is an artist. His photographs have a rythm and a vibration that reflect his love of music; they tell of his faith in God and his love of country. Like his forefathers, Fieguth is a religious man. The Mennonites have a reverence for the soil of Saskatchewan and know the part man must play to protect and preserve it.

Here, then, is a portrait of Saskatchewan. For generations our people have dreamed of opportunity. Now they stand at the threshold of a new era in which those dreams at last may find their realization.

C. Irwin McIntosh
Lieutenant-Governor

1   Foxtail Barley, Battleford

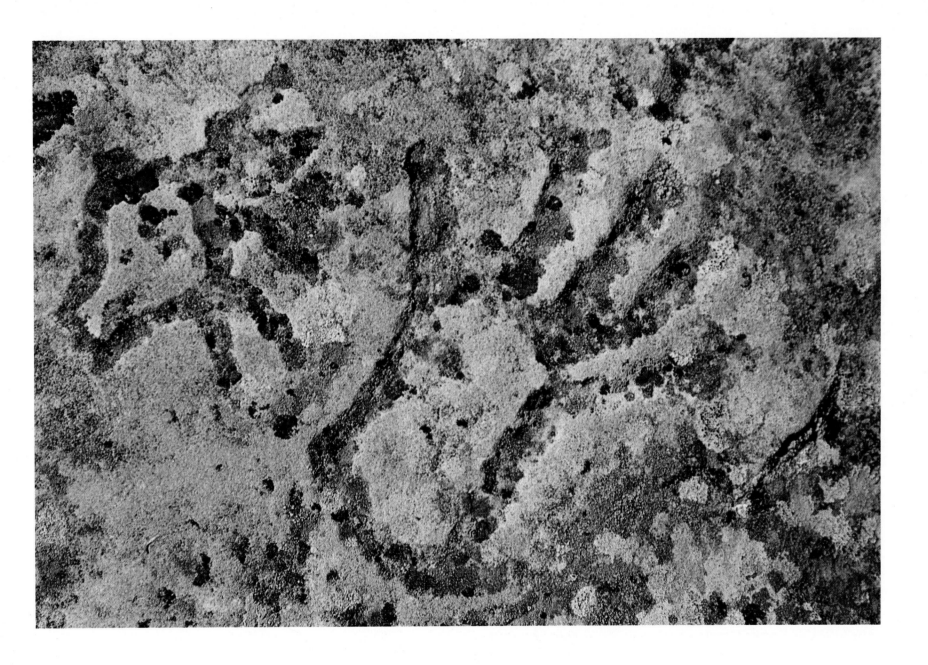

2 Rock formation, Roche Percée
3 Indian rock carving on Buffalo Jump at St Victor

4   Tiger Swallowtail along the Saskatchewan River at Pemmican Portage

5   Aspens at sunset along Hanson Lake Road

10   Lake Athabasca, with sand dunes on the south shore

11   Horses along Battle Creek in the Cypress Hills

12 Farwell's Post, Cypress Hills

13   Al Buziak (as Abe Farwell) at Farwell's Post

14   The cabin of Anaherio (Mrs Grey Owl), near Grey Owl's cabin,
on the shore of Lake Ajawaan

15   Interior of cabin built in 1884 at Cannington Manor

16   Nipikamew Sand Pillars

17   View from Bald Butte in the Cypress Hills

18　Buffalo Jump, with the village of St Victor in the distance

19　The confluence of the North Saskatchewan and Battle Rivers, near the Battlefords

20, 21   Nistowiak Falls, Lac La Ronge Provincial Park

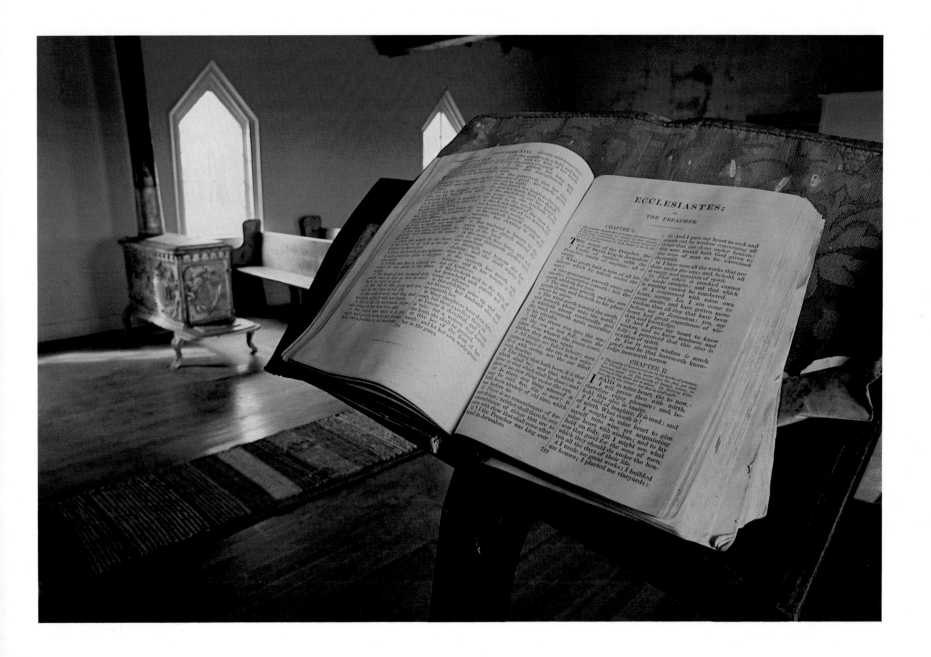

22   Church of the Holy Trinity on the Churchill River at Stanley Mission.
Built in 1856, it is the oldest extant building in Saskatchewan.

23   St Andrew's Anglican Church on the Key Indian Reserve

24 Government House, Battleford, overlooking the Battle River in the morning mist

25 Duck Pond near Battleford

26   Fort Battleford

27   Interior of the Hamlin house, an early French house now in
Pioneer Village, North Battleford

a

b

c

d

28a Western Red Lily, Saskatchewan's floral emblem   29   John Diefenbaker Homestead, Wasana Centre, Regina

28b Sunflower

28c Prairie Crocus

28d Prairie Rose

30   Western Development Museum, Yorkton

31   An old fire engine being demonstrated, Western Development
Museum, Yorkton

32 Engine 6166, Pioneer Village, North Battleford

33a   Outdoor oven, Western Development Museum, Yorkton

33b   Sawing demonstration, Western Development Museum, Yorkton

34   Old binder demonstration,
Western Development Museum,
Yorkton

35   Bundle-pitching competition,
Western Development Museum,
Yorkton

38   Prairie grain elevator, Biggar

39   Kinsmen International
Band Festival, Moose Jaw

40   Great Sand Hills

41   Rape field, Battleford

42   Legislative Building, Regina

43   RCMP Musical Ride, Saskatoon

44 Swift Current

45 Swaths near Battleford

46 Harvesting along the North Saskatchewan River, near Baljennie

47 Near Lancer

48   Weyburn and the Souris River at sunset

49   The Qu'Appelle Valley

a

b

c

d

50a Blueberries, Meadow Lake Provincial Park

50b Reindeer moss

50c Cactus blossoms, Thickwood Hills

50d Mushroom, Meadow Lake Provincial Park

51 The North Saskatchewan River between the Battlefords

52 Survival training at −40°F, Potato Lake, La Ronge

53 La Ronge Winter Festival

54 Courthouse, Weyburn
55 Thunder Hills near Weyakwin

56 Fox Valley

57 South of Maple Creek

58   Bob Keighly, La Ronge
59   La Ronge Winter Festival

60 Stenen

61 Canora

62   Cabin between Eldorado and Uranium City

63   Whitetail deer in the Battle Creek Valley, Cypress Hills

64   Pressure ridge, Lake Athabasca

65a   Mass grave of Métis who fell at Batoche, 1885

65b   Cemetery at Batoche, with Gabriel Dumont's tombstone

66   The Fond du Lac River, with Camp Grayling and Morberg's Camps
67   The William River flowing into Lake Athabasca

68   Creek at the Petrofka Bridge

69a   Grebe on nest, near Battleford

69b   Young gophers (Richardson's Ground Squirrel), Saskatoon

a

b

c

70a   Yellow-headed Blackbird,
Battleford

70b   Pine Grosbeak, Battleford

70c   Shoveler and ducklings, near
Battleford

71   Sailing regatta on Jackfish Lake,
Meota

72 Near Big Muddy
73 Cathedral in Gravelbourg

74 Near Stony Rapids

76a Sculptor Joe Fafard at work in his studio in Pense

76b *Fafard* by Fafard

77 Old-time musicians, Turtleford

78 Farmer's market, Lloydminster

79 Harry Trafford in the La Ronge information booth

80 Ukrainian Welcome Dance, Pioneer Village, North Battleford

81 Ukrainian spinning at the Western Development Museum, North Battleford

82 The North Saskatchewan River near Paynton,
where it is joined by Big Gully Creek

83 Lebret in the Qu'Appelle Valley

84　Athabasca Sand Dunes

85　Potash mine west of Saskatoon

86 Otter Rapids on the historic Churchill River

87 Saskatoon

▷88 Thunderstorm, Eagle Hills